TRUTH

Rocky Evans

edited by Georgia Pieper-Outman

iUniverse, Inc.
Bloomington

TRUTH

Copyright © 2011 by Rocky Evans

All rights reserved. No part of this book may be used or reproduced by any means, graphic, electronic, or mechanical, including photocopying, recording, taping or by any information storage retrieval system without the written permission of the publisher except in the case of brief quotations embodied in critical articles and reviews.

iUniverse books may be ordered through booksellers or by contacting:

iUniverse
1663 Liberty Drive
Bloomington, IN 47403
www.iuniverse.com
1-800-Authors (1-800-288-4677)

Because of the dynamic nature of the Internet, any web addresses or links contained in this book may have changed since publication and may no longer be valid. The views expressed in this work are solely those of the author and do not necessarily reflect the views of the publisher, and the publisher hereby disclaims any responsibility for them.

Any people depicted in stock imagery provided by Thinkstock are models, and such images are being used for illustrative purposes only.

Certain stock imagery © Thinkstock.

ISBN: 978-1-4620-6615-5 (sc)
ISBN: 978-1-4620-6616-2 (e)

Printed in the United States of America

iUniverse rev. date: 11/14/2011

This Book is dedicated to Ken Coleman, my teammate and friend, who perished in the balloon crash.

This Book is also dedicated to my parents, Robert and Betty Evans, who lovingly raised me and taught me the skills and values that have carried me through life.

Special thanks to Claire Pieper for her support and for providing me with the perfect writer's environment.

Special thanks to Georgia Pieper-Outman. Without her co-writing, encouragement and belief in me this story may never have been written.

Barrington Hills, IL Air Balloon Crash Kills Five, Aug 1981

Posted June 20th, 2008 by Stu Beitler

FIVE KILLED IN CRASH OF AIR BALLOON.

"Five people were killed and a sixth was critically injured in a fiery crash Saturday night when a birthday trip in a hot-air balloon ended in tragedy after the balloon smashed into high-voltage power lines in Barrington Hills and exploded in flames.

The lone survivor jumped from the balloon and landed on the median strip of Route 14 at Kelsey Road after a fall of as much as 100 feet, Lake County Sheriff's police said. HARRY EVANS, 29, of De Land, Fla., was in critical but stable condition in the burn unit of Evanston Hospital with burns over 25 percent of his body."

According to the above article, three other passengers of the balloon ride were found at the crash site, but were burned beyond recognition. The two remaining victims had also jumped from the balloon, but did not survive. Ken Coleman jumped to his death from an unknown altitude. The sixth victim also jumped, but did not survive through the day with third and fourth degree burns over 90 percent of his body.

The trip was originally scheduled for a few weeks earlier, and was a birthday present from the pilot to one of the passengers. It was postponed due to poor weather and rescheduled for August 16th. The balloon appeared to be attempting to land due to poor weather, according to some witnesses. One witness, who owned a nearby restaurant, thought a gust of wind blew the balloon into high-tension wires. The top of the utility pole was broken and there was a power outage after the balloon hit the wires.

The article also stated that Evans leaped out of the balloon when it hit the utility pole and then the balloon continued south, and that is when a second passenger jumped out and landed in a field. This was Ken Coleman, who apparently died upon impact. According to officials, a third passenger also jumped out and crashed through a roof of a house.

TRUTH

My good friend, Ken Coleman, and I arrived at the Windy City Balloon Port, Barrington Hills at about 12:00 noon. We started our class at 1:00 o'clock. Ken was giving the lecture and I was assisting him. This lecture covered the basic instruction for the AFF Course (Accelerated Free Fall). We discussed the equipment, emergencies, dive flow and canopy control, etc. This class was unique in that we were instructing balloon pilots for the first time.

Following the afternoon class one of the balloon pilots, Jamie B., invited us on a balloon ride he had planned for later that evening. It was a belated birthday present for his friend. They intended to go several weeks earlier, but storms delayed the birthday excursion. Now this was the largest balloon in the world and it carried six people. Ken said that he would go and I guess he felt obligated since Jamie was the one who got us the contract to teach the AFF course. We were both pretty tired and had hoped to just kick back for the rest of the evening. After all, we had driven seven hours that morning prior to teaching the course. Ken kept saying, "C'mon let's go. It's free." Man! I was really tired and had been looking forward to taking a shower, relaxing with a cold beer and settling in for the evening. Ken said to me, under his breath, "C'mon Rocky. These people are going out of their way to show us a good time, so let's go." Well, I went.

We approached the launch site. This was the largest basket (gondola) I had ever seen, and it carried six passengers. The launch site looked like a giant sinkhole. I guessed it was probably a perfect place to launch a balloon because it was protected from the wind. I watched as Ken and Jamie used the burner to fill the balloon with fuel for the liftoff. This balloon was twice the size of the one that I skydived from in the Florida Keys. I was feeling some loss of energy from what already seemed to be a long day, and more or less was a spectator and did as I was told. Jamie was the 'pilot in command' on this trip. When it came time for us to climb aboard, I recall there were three other men who got in the basket with us.

I never did get their names, but I assumed one of them was the "birthday boy". After we were all on board, Jamie hit the burner and the balloon inflated until it was full and round. Then the ground crew let go of the ropes that held us in place. The balloon shot up like it was full of helium. There it wavered, big and full, wanting to fly but held back by the tether lines. It reminded me of a stallion horse that had just been roped by a lasso, trying with all its might to break free. I waited inside the gondola, contemplating where we might be going. Little did I know that the entire world would hear about that twenty-minute flight on the evening news.

Suddenly this guy came running toward us yelling, "Wait! Wait! Don't forget this!" He had the customary bottle of champagne for the traditional toast at the end of the flight. Jamie placed it on the floor of the gondola, next to the large propane tanks. Now these tanks weren't the little tanks that you use for your gas grill, no, these two tanks were almost three times the size of gas grill propane tanks. Remember, this was the largest hot air balloon in the world.

Finally, we were off! The tether lines were released and we lifted up and out of that 'dirt bowl' nature had made for the balloon launch. I was a little concerned, because in the distance I spotted the black horizon associated with a thunderstorm. Similar to my first balloon ride, I noticed the silence of the ride – only broken by the power of the burner. We were moving along at a pretty good pace, not like an airplane or a helicopter, but definitely faster than a person walking. I would say we were going as fast as if I were running. We never climbed any higher than seventy-five to one hundred feet. Now I am of the belief that bad things happen in threes: **Number one** – the pilot, aware that the weather conditions weren't favorable, made the choice to launch. We are already up and flying and in the distance I could see a thunderstorm starting to grow. Admittedly, it was pretty far off in the distance, but I was thinking that it *would* become an issue. I didn't say anything.

As we quietly soared close to the ground, I was looking down into the neighborhood yards, listening to the dogs barking at the Big Air Monster that hissed fire. Jamie kept our altitude low and at one point we hit an antenna, the gondola slightly rocked as we glanced off of it. **Number two** – why didn't Jamie climb to a higher altitude to avoid this careless flying? It was at this point that I started to question his skill level. Ken said he was a highly skilled balloonist with many flights under his belt. Why didn't he see the antenna? Why?! No one said a thing…the unusual silence continued. I looked at the strangers, the novices, and wondered what they were thinking. Perhaps this was their first balloon ride and they were clueless. The balloon was picking up speed as we raced along.

My mind went back to my first balloon ride from which I skydived, but that ride was at two thousand feet – not as "up close and personal" to the ground as this ride. I was remembering what a pain it was to climb up and out of that gondola in order to jump. Hell, the side of the basket is chest-high and there is no door on these baskets. The way the gondolas are made, there is nothing to grab onto once you are outside of it. There are carrying handles, made of wicker like the basket, but they are down at the base of the basket. I realized I was already thinking about a way out. I must have known, deep inside, of the imminent danger. I began to consciously think about a crash landing, and had lost my confidence in the pilot. I knew if we hit the ground at our current speed, the gondola would start to roll. The last thing I wanted was to get knocked in the head with one of those large propane tanks, or to get tangled up with the others in the basket! Then the first words on that flight were spoken. Jamie said, with an undertone of panic, "I'm going to land the balloon. The weather is looking bad and I feel that we need to land." I looked directly into his face as he spoke his words and I saw an undeniable expression of panic and question. I did not like what I saw. "Damn it!", I thought. "Why in the *hell* did I go!? I *knew* I should have stayed on the ground! Too late, damn it, *too late!*"

Off in the distance was a large asphalt parking lot. Jamie pointed and said that was where we were going to land. "Shit!" I thought, "On the asphalt? That's gonna hurt!" Why in the hell he chose that point I don't know, because on the other side were power wires. These were not small ones, they were large power wires – the kind that had big steel-framed girders that looked like a large "T". Beyond the wires were large, open fields. Why did he not choose that spot? What was he thinking?! Now here's this hotshot balloon pilot who had logged thousands of hours of flight. I never thought there was much skill involved. All you really do is run the burner for lift, and pull a tether line up to the top of the envelope (balloon). This line is hooked to one side of a big opening at the very apex of the balloon. When you pull down it lets out hot air that collected at the top. When you are in flight, you pull down on the tether line and you open up the envelope. Once the apex is open, it releases the hot air and the balloon starts to descend. The longer it's open, the quicker you descend. Also, the longer it's open the more time it takes to respond. At this point I'm really starting to get concerned. We are moving along at a pretty good clip and the parking lot is coming up closer and closer. We are not that high, maybe fifty feet or so. Jamie pulls the tether down, and then down again to the basket floor. We were just about to hit the parking lot, maybe six feet from the asphalt – *six feet*, the average height of a man – when he released the tether, closing the envelope and hit the burner for lift. He aborted the landing! My God! We were *so close....so damn close!!* All of us – all six of us could've climbed out of that gondola, but he chose to **abort!?** Why? Why?! It made no sense! **Number three.**

The noise of the burner started to roar. We hit something and the gondola turned 180°. There we were – motionless – as if God Himself was holding our gondola in His almighty hands. Time stood still during that moment of unworldly suspension – that sudden, unexplainable cessation of movement. My mind was racing through possible scenarios! What in the *hell!?! I looked down! We were definitely NOT moving!* We must have been STUCK!!! 'Stuck?!?! On WHAT?!?! We were in the frigging sky for God's sake! Wait! Is it another antenna?!' Then it hit me! 'THE POWER WIRES! THE GOD DAMN POWER WIRES!' At that moment I knew! I knew from my skydiving career that we were just plain *screwed!* Instinctively, I crouched into the corner of the gondola. Here I was, wearing my favorite hat that Jerry Bird gave me, a cotton polyester shirt, Levi jeans and tennis shoes. I can still see those three strangers standing up looking over the edge of the basket, as if they were passengers on an ocean liner looking at the massive sea below. To this day I do not recall seeing Ken or talking to him.

So here I was, crouched in the corner of this gondola, and I knew, I *really knew* how screwed I was. Time, again, was our real enemy – the amount of time we had from the gondola coming into contact with the first wire – until it involved the second wire. As long as we were hooked on just one wire, we were safe. Now listen carefully....because this is where the story differs from all prior written accounts. This is where the **TRUTH** is exposed from deep inside the sole survivor of the largest hot air balloon crash in world history in 1981.

When the wind hit the massive balloon, it created a lot of drag. Now picture this gondola caught on the wire. Where exactly was this wire? It was just below the top lip where you climb into the basket. If you were to look over the edge of the basket, it would be a foot below you. I was in the corner, my hands covering the top of my head and my arms in front of my face. I was peering in between my arms, still not sure of my fate. I recall asking myself, "Why am I here? What have I done in my life to be here? Have I been that bad of a person to wind up here facing death?" I knew my answer was 'no'. Since I was a child I had believed in this thing called God. Then my mind went to all of my childhood friends who had died...Steven W., Tommy S., Tom M., Mary W. Tony, Ron. This wasn't a new place, hell, not at all! I stared it in the face so many times, I guess I was used to it – that place everyone eventually goes.

I can honestly tell you that I knew, and I mean I *truly knew* that we were about to die. I was sure that the pilot, Jamie, also knew. Ken had to have known. I felt sorry for the three passengers. They had no idea of what lay ahead of them. They were like little babies, unaware of how bad fire was. They did not have the training, experience, and more so, the knowledge that comes with skydiving. I knew that when you come into contact with power wires, that is the VERY WORST of all emergency landings. You are told to keep your hands over your face and turn your head away from the fire. The last I saw, the three passengers were peering over the edge of the basket at the power wire that had snagged us. I'm sure they were totally unaware of what to expect. In those *brief* moments I knew what the outcome would be! The dreaded moment came, and come it did, with more fire and intense heat than anyone has ever experienced and lived to tell the story!

I have kept this inside of me for all these years – bottled up – only to come out in the late hours of my sleep. I guess you could call them nightmares. I could not talk about this horrific tragedy. It wasn't even a choice….I just could not talk about it. Here, deep inside of me, is where this deadly disaster has remained for the past thirty years. Why is it now coming out? Why am I able to tell the details now?

How is it possible for me to re-live this story of death at this point in my life? I am not sure, but I do know that it began to seep and now it pours out of me and I must not try to hold it back.

Again, I was down in the corner of the basket, hands covering the top of my head, arms covering my face and suddenly there was a simultaneous *blinding* flash of light, *intense* heat and an *ungodly loud* sound penetrating the sky! It was bright – so bright! The heat was so intense, it is unimaginable! When those two power lines came together it was a sound that still stays locked in my brain. It wasn't like the sound of a welder as he strikes an arc with his rod. It wasn't like the noise you hear when you have two 110AC wires on an appliance or even the sound you may have heard if a transformer blew. No, this was the sound of <u>death</u>. It roared with a noise of extreme, inhuman power. This brief period of time – from when the wires erupted into the merciless flash, heat and roar, until I jumped – was no more than one or two seconds.

My last vision, the one I still see, was that of the three passengers looking over the side of the balloon. I can only imagine what happened to them when the two 34,000-volt power wires touched in their deadly kiss. I know the damage it did to me, and I was ready for the fiery monster that was unleashed. I remember thinking, "God, I'm burning! I'm really going to burn to death!" As I look back, I realize my life never did flash before my eyes as others say they experienced. For a moment I accepted it, I relented – 'death, let it come'. It almost felt like peace...finally peace. "Maybe", I thought, "this is where I will see the other side."

In an instant I found myself being propelled out of the gondola! The heat was *so intense I could not take it any longer!* Somehow my strong legs powered me up and out of that basket in one motion! As I look back, I know my survival instinct took over – I do not recall consciously deciding to jump. I was in free fall, feet first, arms stretched out from my sides making small circles to help me balance. My form was as perfect as it could be – vertical, not bending, feet first. I did not know my final destiny. How could I? There was no time to look down to see where I would land. I guess I didn't care. All I knew was that I was released from that intense heat and out of that burning coffin. Now from one hundred feet you can get a good free fall. I am really not sure how long I was falling, but it was long enough for me to focus on my body position. I hit the ground and instinctively went into a PLF (parachute landing fall). I immediately began rolling, my skydiving experience in auto-mode, and as I rolled I began to pick up speed to where I was tumbling head-over-heels, faster and faster. I recall rolling into, up and over a large tree-like bush and *still* continued to roll. Sand, dirt, grass and leaves were being shoved into my mouth and face. I was so disoriented I couldn't believe it. I was a living bowling ball rolling out of control.

Finally, it stopped – finally. Still alive, I wondered if I broke my legs. I cautiously stood up. I was amazed that I did not break my legs! I looked at myself. The skin on my arms was dangling in small clumps, and my hands looked as if they were dipped in warm clear wax. I looked at my left hand. It was upside down! My arm was out straight, and my palm was facing up! I looked at my right arm and the palm was facing the ground. Then there was that stench in my nostrils – the burning hair and flesh – <u>*my* *smoldering hair and flesh!*</u> Most of us have smelled burning hair, but the stench of burning flesh cannot even be described. I realized that the cool hat Jerry Bird gave me was gone. My shirt was burned into my skin, and the only remaining part was the neckline. I recall thinking, "My God! My body is <u>smoking</u>!!" The rancid odor of my own skin and hair was making me sick!

Again, this "time thing" comes into play. I don't know how long it was from the time I quit rolling down that huge hill until the time it was when I stood up. I really do not know! I do know that after I stood up and saw that my legs were not broken, I ran – and I mean *ran* – up this hill! My adrenalin was really pumping. I must have been in shock, because I was pretty burned up but did not feel burned. Once I made it to the top of the hill, it was only a few more yards until I was in the road trying to flag down someone – *anyone* – to get help for the people in the gondola. When I got to the top of the hill I saw the balloon. "My God!", I recall thinking. The side of the actual basket was on fire! The frigging gondola itself was burning! Flames were pouring from the top of the gondola, and as I write this I now have figured out exactly *what* was on fire! In my mind I remember flames, large ones pouring out the side of the gondola. These flames were reaching up fifteen feet, melting the side of the balloon. The gondola was producing the flames! The damn wicker was on fire! That's it! The gondola must have hit the tall pole that spun us 180° and that was the first contact with the power wire – that side of the basket – right where the poor three passengers were. As I write this I now realize that was right where *I would have been,* had the gondola not spun from the pole. Yes, *now* it is coming together in my mind. Here the basket was, caught on the power line, and the balloon, unable to rise, was beginning to blow sideways. Picture a rabbit in a snare, lunging and jerking to get free. This movement pushed the first wire into the second and the result was deadly. Once the wires were severed due to the contact, the balloon was free in its skyward quest. The flaming gondola added *additional* fuel to the fire, causing the death coffin to rise even more quickly.

There I stood, watching this death trap descend like a bird, its wing shot in flight, spiraling down to the earth below. I could only think, "My God, Ken, I hope he got out." I knew, I just knew he had escaped that burning coffin. I watched it crash into the yard of someone's house. My mind was racing as I stood motionless, watching this god-awful sight. There I stood with my skin-dripping body, upside down hand, and the putrid odor of dead hair and skin permeating the air.

Looking back, I realize I was in shock because I recall my mind was drifting to thoughts of the hot air balloon. "This airship is as old as flight itself. The very first time man ever left the chains of gravity was in an envelope full of hot air. If you look in the history books about the introduction of manned flight, there it will be in its entirety. The conception of the hot air balloon – unlike the airplane. The power plant of the hot air balloon has not changed – unlike the mechanical aspect of the gasoline engine. Hot air and its properties have not changed. Not only that, but the means to make the fuel for hot air balloons has not changed either. That fuel is **fire**."

I watched as the balloon came down, closer and closer to the ground. At last, gravity and the loss of power caused it to crash. It burst into the biggest ball of fire I had ever seen! One moment it was there, the next it was gone, as if a magician had waved his magic wand. Gone – yet never gone from my mind – a vision I will never be able to wave away with a wand. Then there was the question. The question anyone in my position would've asked. "Is anyone else alive?"

The vision of those last few moments in that inferno come back to me night after night in a dream – a nightmare – one of death and sorrow that I never want to see again. Like a damn skipping record, it comes back, night after night, haunting me – always beginning with Ken's face, both of us in the basket, the basket on fire and Ken grabbing for me, pulling me back and saying, "No! No! Don't jump! You will be killed!" Next the three passengers are looking over the edge of the basket and they slowly turn to me. I see their grotesque melting faces, as they are reaching out for me, *touching* me with their skinless hands and then voices somewhere from within their steaming bodies pleading, "No! No! Don't jump!" I awaken in a sweat! My heart is racing! My bed covers are a total mess! The dream still comes to me as I am sure it will for the rest of my life. God! It will never go away!

People would later ask me why I didn't tell everyone to jump. These people just did not understand! The thought of jumping did not come to mind! In a moment such as that, had it even come to mind, it would have taken way too long. This moment I am describing, is like no other moment in your life. No one knows what a **'moment'** of this circumstance really is, or how long this moment will *last...if at all*....until that person experiences it as **I** did. <u>I have been there, yet I cannot fully explain it.</u> No one, and I can truly say this....*no one* knows how time can kill you or how time can save you, until *you, <u>only</u> you have survived this experience.* Until then, you will not understand.

I stood there thinking how no one could possibly survive that ball of fire I just witnessed. One minute it was there – the next minute it was gone. The pain was beginning to grab me, and it was weird how it progressed and intensified through my body in stages. An elderly couple stopped their car and approached me. They encouraged me to lie down in the back seat of their car. I said "No, no! I can't find my friend who was in that balloon and I need to get help!" They pleaded with me to lie down in their car and I responded with a definite "no".

The pain was becoming intense. I knew it was over and there was nothing I could do. I looked at my freakish upside down hand, the melted skin dripping off my arms and hands, and was becoming sick to my stomach from my own rancid odor. I succumbed to the kind elderly couple's offer of shelter and rest. Time now stood still, like being in a bubble. Sirens were beginning to scream louder and louder as they approached. I found myself feeling badly about the stains and odor I would leave in the old couple's car, and apologized to them. They were so concerned and caring and here I was making a mess of their back seat. I remember thinking of the

AFF program, and Ken. "God! Where's Ken? Did he make it? I did, maybe he did too." I don't know how long I lay there, but long enough to begin to feel the tremendous pain from the burns all over my body. At first my broken hand was my only concern. I was not looking forward to the doctor resetting it. I began to take notice of the damage to my arms and hands. My God! The skin was dripping off my entire hand and arm, all the way up to where my shirt sleeve was. Then I looked at my right arm and it was worse – a lot worse! I looked at my legs and they were burned also, but I only saw a few big spots where my skin was gone. My entire body began shaking as if I was having a seizure! My mind was still solid, I never really lost it, at least in my opinion.

An ambulance pulled up to the car and the EMT's appeared in front of me with a stretcher. They tried to grab me and I pulled away from them telling them not to touch me that I would get on the stretcher myself. Their hands on my open wounds increased my pain! Once inside the ambulance they began to ask me questions. I understood the reason for all the questions, but my pain was intensifying and I couldn't focus. My wrist was really hurting! It is odd how the two – my broken wrist and the burns

– emitted different sensations of pain. The big relief was the sensation of the water they were pouring over my body. The pain was becoming *unbearable!* I begged them to give me something for it! The EMT's said they couldn't give me anything. It was almost dark by the time we reached the hospital.

I'm looking up at the ceiling as I'm being quickly rolled to a hospital room. Here I am, lying on this gurney, alone in this room, in the worst pain I have ever felt, and I hear myself chuckle.

….I made it! I hurt. Where's Ken? I hurt. I wonder….I hurt….I wait…I hurt…come on! Get me something for the pain! I wait…At last a nurse! She's got a syringe…I get something for the pain….I hurt….I moan….I hurt. Another nurse is here…Oh, not for me. Oh! Somebody else is here…she's closing the curtain…metal curtain holders being scraped along the rod…..I can't see who it is….someone else in our party made it?! Ken! I *knew* he got out! Doctor's here….finally!….he's gonna set this wrist…I know what the hell's going on….

The doctor comes to me and picks up my arm. "H-m-m-m", he says. My hand is still dripping, every finger and thumb has skin dripping off of it. The smell is terrible! I can't touch a thing, and I don't want anyone to touch me. "Where's Ken?",

I ask. Doc says, "Who?" "Ken, he's my friend who was with me in the balloon. Is he dead?", I ask. "I don't know", Doc says, "I'm going to set this wrist. How's the pain?" I tell him, "Bad! Terrible!!" He leaves. My mind goes back to the partition. I'm going to see if that's Ken in the room next to me, but I can't get up off the bed.

....I hurt....here comes the nurse again....good! She's got a syringe! Give me more – MORE!....go ahead, stick me in my butt cheek....just GIVE me something for this goddamn pain!....she's gone...I hurt....I hear voices in the next room....more than two....that's gotta be Ken....I *knew* he made it....here comes the doctor....

"How's the pain?" he asks again. I tell him it's better. "I'm gonna set this now, you ready?", he says. "I've been ready", I respond. I keep smelling that damn stink – burned hair and flesh! I look down and my frigging shoes are burned and full of dirt. I figure I must have gotten that when I ran up the hill. My Levi jeans are burned, my arms have dirt all over them, sticking to the skinless parts. My hands are the worst! I can still see the loose, hanging pieces of skin. My shirt was the best – cotton polyester with melted pieces sticking to the good pieces on my back, chest and arms. My back and shoulders are burned pretty bad and even my ears are burned. My right ear is the worst. God! My hair's burned off. The doctor now has my arm in his hand. He says, "This is going to hurt'. I tell him, "I know, do it!" He's sitting in a chair, facing me, and he stands up and grabs hold of my hand. He starts to pull, and I scream as he twists my hand – he keeps twisting and I keep screaming! He lets go, the twisting stops, and my hand is right side up. "Yahoo !" I cheer. Doc looks at me and smiles, and I look up at him and smile and thank him. He nods and leaves the room.

....I hurt....

Time is gone. There is no time, it doesn't exist. I feel the bright lights beating down on me. Two nurses enter my room carrying stainless steel pans on a stainless steel tray. I'm still wondering about Ken. I ask them, "Where's Ken?" The nurses tell me they are going to cut off my shirt and I say, "Great". I'm not hurting as bad, the morphine is starting to work. They ask me if I can sit up. I sit up and they begin cutting. God! That nasty odor is terrible! I wonder if it will ever go away! I ask the nurses who's in the other bed and they say they don't know. They keep cutting. The pieces are burned and melted into my body. They're doing a good job. The burned pieces are dropping to the floor. My mind goes back to the burning balloon fluttering down. I ask them when I can find out about my friend and they tell me they don't know. ….I hurt…. they put moist, wet cloths on my back. It feels good. The remnants of the shirt are almost completely removed. Patches of it are still stuck to my raw flesh. My pants are next. Fortunately, they're not as bad as the polyester shirt. I think back to Ken. He was wearing polyester pants. I know how they must look. The nurses begin bathing my wounds and it feels good.

Two men enter my room. "Harry Evans?", they inquire. "Yes", I respond. "We have bad news. Ken is dead." "Well, that's that", I say. It surely wasn't a shock. They tell me he jumped after I did, but he jumped from a higher altitude and did not survive. I ask them who is in the room next to me. They tell me it's one of the passengers who also jumped, and landed on top of a house. "My God!", I'm thinking. I found out later that he landed on top of the roof and crashed though it. The poor guy must have really been broken.

They transport me to another hospital that is better equipped for severe burn victims. At this point, things are not real clear and I'm sure the morphine is taking its toll. The next morning I awaken to a flock of nurses. One is trying to stick me with an I.V. and another is putting a tube down my nose and into my stomach. They also put a catheter in my penis. The I.V. is hanging from my jugular vein in my neck! Then, if this isn't enough, they are trying to make me sit up so they can change my bandages. Good luck! I am stuck to my sheets and am not able to get up from the bed. The nurses soak the bed and now I am able to tear free and sit up. I am thinking, "If that's what it takes just to get me up, what the hell will it take to get these bandages off?" They soak me down and wait twenty minutes or so and then they start removing my bandages. I'm feeling real dizzy. I float in and out of the dreamy world of morphine. The morphine does so much, but the pain is still present – deadened in a dull way, but it stays with me for weeks.

OK, bandages off and I figure they will clean the burns with a solution and put fresh bandages on me. WRONG! It's 8:00 am and I see they are here to take me somewhere. I listen. The nurses are talking about a debris tank. I know nothing of what they are speaking. We are moving and it takes three of them to transport me – one to push the gurney, one to keep me from falling off and one to carry the stuff that I'm hooked up to. I am wondering what is in store for me now. They roll me into this room with a large whirlpool tank. At least that is what it looks like. I remember using one in high school when I tore up my knee in football. I used to get out of study hall to go down into the locker room to use the whirlpool tank. Man! I thought I was somebody special – get out of class to sit and relax and help my knee heal. I chose not to have surgery, as I would not have been able to play football my senior year. Hell, all I could do was punt, but it was my forte and I was good – good enough to be considered by Michigan State.

This tank has a fold outside and it's a good thing. It is a painful struggle to get in this thing with burns all over and dragging all the apparatus that's plugged into me. They shot me with extra morphine, but I still feel pain. Once I'm in, damn does it feel good! A motor is stirring the water, and bubbles are whirling around. I just get good and relaxed, and seem to be feeling less pain for the first time since I escaped from the fiery coffin, and a new nurse walks in. I greet her and tell her my name and she tells me hers. She says she is going to clean my burns, and I see this damn stiff bristle brush in her hand. I'm thinking, with dreaded concern, "What the hell is she gonna do with *that* damn brush?" My question is answered all too soon. She begins *scrubbing my open wounds* with that god-awful bristle brush! Dear God! I cannot *bear* this unimaginable pain! For Christ's sake! Is this the way these people bathe RAW SKIN!?!?! She scrubs and scrubs and I see the whirlpool water changing to a bloody hue. I am screaming! Crying! Cursing! It's all in vain....this devil in nurse's garb does not stop the torture until she has attacked every wound – a torture that lasts for one and a half hours. Every now and then she stops to change her brush and clean my wounds of dead skin and plastic, remnants of my shirt burned into my body. I pass out. When I regain consciousness she tells me that it's OK, a lot of her patients pass out and it's good so they don't have to feel the pain.

When will this be over?! She finally says that the worst is over and I am done. Oh my God! My body burns way, *way* more than that first burning sensation in the balloon! The two nurses who brought me here are now coating me with Silvedene and putting fresh bandages on me. I am being rolled back to my room. I tell them, "Damn, I'm sure glad that's done." They reply telling me it is one of the most painful things I will experience here. I say, "No shit! I'm sure glad that's done!" The one nurse said, "Yes, I bet, but you need to know that they are going to do this to you again at 3 o'clock this afternoon and then again at 8 o'clock tonight." "**WHAT**? For how long?!?!?" She replied, "Every day until you leave."

....What can I do?!? How can I escape this daily hell? *I cannot escape!! My God ....please help me!*

I get a roommate after a few days. His name is Jimmy and he's about ten years old. Poor Jimmy, he is the victim of extreme childhood brutality. Some older kids, around twelve or thirteen, threw gasoline on this little guy and set him on fire. Jimmy and I become good friends. I never do see his face because his head is always covered in a Jove stocking, with only his eyes and mouth visible. His face, head, arms and hands are badly burned. I heard someone say it was 50% of his body. He is such a good boy. Jimmy's parents come to visit daily, and since I have no one near to visit me; I start to feel like they are my family too.

I am in Evanston, Illinois – some distance from my little hometown of Three Rivers, Michigan. That's where I was born and raised – just a little mid-western town of farmers, factories and local businesses. The town was divided into four wards – the nicer neighborhoods were in first ward, second ward homes were a little less nice, then third ward. Well – you get the gist. Me? I grew up in fourth ward, but you know how I looked at it? I figured four was the highest number – how many dollars do you want – one or four? Yeah, that's how I looked at it. Well, society eventually poisoned my childhood optimism. I slowly became aware of the favorable way first ward residents were treated compared to the less affluent residents of the descending wards. Fourth ward folks weren't worthy of respect like first ward snobs? Give me a break! *Society* – who were they?! The parents – and the parents of the parents. So, now these kids in Three Rivers are learning early on of their "worthiness" in frigging society? I wonder what ward little Jimmy is from.

Most of the black people lived in second and fourth ward. My best friend was a black kid named Doochee – well, that's what he was called anyway. Many nights he slept over at my house – hell, we slept in the same bed! We didn't care about color, that never came to mind! Different? Segregation? We never heard those words, at least not in those naive, innocent days of our youth. Our parents certainly didn't act any different, regardless of who we played with. Things were simple back then. We were best buddies and loved each other the way two young boys learning about friendship do. Friend?! You couldn't have asked for a better friend than Doochee, and I gave him that same friendship right back. I continue to cherish many friendships, regardless of their money **or** color.

It's just a sad thing that society continues to pigeon-hole people by their wealth. I have found that many well-to-do people are phony, or "plastic" as I like to call them. There are a few who are down to earth, but very few. The majority of these "first warders" are pretentious – and you know, I never thought they were very happy. Too bad it takes so much money to be able to get recognized in the political world. We end up with "first warders" running our country. What a choice for the voters! Is it a wonder why many just don't vote? What the hell? Which plastic politician shall we choose this term?!

….damn morphine….makes my mind drift all over the place….why the hell am I thinking about that shit?!….

I never got into morphine – I did dabble with cocaine a little. I tried heroin once or twice, and it was just like they said it would be – an indescribable euphoric sensation. After the first time, though, that level of euphoria could never be duplicated with subsequent use.

Now here I lay – a victim of my own passion and devotion to skydiving. Twenty-nine years old and there is nothing else that I would rather do. At first it was for sport, but now I know that we are dedicated to improving and enhancing the sport to new levels never before achieved. Hell – never before imagined for all Ken and I know. We didn't even finish our lecture on Accelerated Free Fall! My good friend, Ken, is dead. Me, I'm – how did they put it? – "critical". The morphine is being pumped into me by the hour and I lie here like a zombie. Drool runs from the corners of my mouth, and I feel as if I'm a mentally challenged person with no control over his body. I barely have control over my mind as it drifts in and out of reality.

The time in this room is like heaven and hell. At last, relieved of the relentless pain, I lie in medicated tolerance, dressed in my pure white bandages. I am calmed with the floating thought of being one of Jesus Christ's disciples. Then I am brought back into harsh reality – abruptly separated from that peaceful place, and again experiencing pain as my flesh is being separated from the crusty bed where the tears of my wounds wept. My bandages are removed and my open wounds throb with pain as the air bites them. All too soon I am being transported, against my will, to Lucifer's special room. I learn it is of no use to fight – the baptismal from hell has no soul.

In my more lucid moments I tell myself that I *must* get well. The only way to end this misery, is to get well. I yearn to see out of the windows, but the curtains are drawn tight! They say the sun must be avoided, that the UV rays will harm my healing skin. Meanwhile, I don't know if it's day or night, Monday or Saturday, or how long I have lay in this zombie-like state.

….yeah, here she comes with the morphine…. go ahead, let it flow through me….keep me in this mental fog….keep me placated so I won't try to escape from the journeys to Lucifer….

One minute I am talking to this nurse and the next I "wake up" and there is no nurse. I wonder if she was really there or if it was another "morphine mirage."

1970-Rocky's first demo jump –Three Rivers, Michigan

1974 - Rocky in formation – Zephyrhills. Florida

SKYDIVING CHAMPIONS — The Rainbow Flyers, a parachuting team based in nearby Athens, Michigan, won the United States National Championships in Tallequah, Oklahoma, in July and will compete in the First World Relative Work Championships in From the left: Ken Cole Carpenter, and a US off

1974 – World Meet – Receiving their medals. (Photo from *Three Rivers Commercial-News*)

CHAMPION JUMPERS — Black and white doesn't do justice to the colorful outfits worn by the Rainbow Flyers, parachute jumping team, which took the world championship at Warendorf, Germany, recently. Rocky Evans, left, wears a royal blue and yellow jump suit, and holds a brilliant yellow chute. Fellow team-mates, from left to right, Ken Coleman, Don Carpenter, and Sam Brown, wear red and white. Next goal of the team is the World Cup Competition in South Africa.

Rainbow Flyers – Champion jumpers took the world championship in Warendorf, Germany. (Photo from *Three Rivers Commercial-News*)

1974 – World Championship – "Rainbow Flyers" – Pretoria, South Africa

Taking the little white dog on a skydive

1984 – Rocky and the Steerman

First sheet metal work with John Simon's ex-WWII sheet metal guy

Rocky and the Steerman

Rocky sitting at his desk where he owned and operated Flagler Aviation - 1990 - 1999

1991 -Rocky in his C-206 with the French 4-way Girls Team

1991 –Rocky, Fang and the French Team. Rocky built the jump door and step on the plane

1986 – Cierra Autana – Rocky and Ernesto

1986 – Cierra Autana - Rocky was flying the 206 "chase plane" from which this photo was taken

Rocky at campsite - Autana

1986 - Rocky washing up among carnivorous plants

Cierra Autana – Rocky tandem parachuted onto this small monolith surface

After landing, Rocky collapses his parachute due to the fast ground wind

Skydiving practice out of a DC-3 over Puerto Ayachucho

Flagler Skydive Team

1996 – Rocky takes his Flagler Skydiving Team down to Providenciales in the Turks and Caicos Islands to do a tandem school. They completed 233 tandem jumps in 13 days.

....what time is it....where's the damn clock....I hurt....when will this stop....I'm getting stuck to my bed again....I can't turn....I just wanna change positions....blood and clear fluid leaking again....what is that shit....god I'm a prisoner to my own seeping body....soon the nasty ooze will turn into glue and pin me to the bed....

The nurses come with spray bottles of water, squirt me down, and dissolve the dried leakage. I sigh with relief. My eyes go to Jimmy and I feel ashamed for being selfish about my discomfort. There he is, my "masked friend", already exposed to trauma far worse than anything I had experienced at that age. I am in this room because of a sporting accident – a combination of poor decisions, including my decision to join the ride. Jimmy? This little guy is here because he was the target of extreme bullying and hatred. His burns are the result of judgment – mine, on the other hand, are the result of misjudgment.

Man! I would give *anything* for a glass of water. They tell me I can't have water, because I will lose even more protein out of my wounds. My mind drifts back to the cold water that came out of our old pump on my grandparents' farm. Dad and I would go down to the old pump house to get that cold drink. It was an old shack made of red barn wood. A concrete tank lay with a 3/4" pipe coming out of the shack. It was a typical old shack door held closed with a piece of wood and a nail through the center of it, to allow it to swing in and out of the latch. Inside the shack is where the old motor and pump were. They put straw all over the bottom floor to help keep it from freezing. The old wires came up to a switch that led to two copper connections. It made me think of the lever Dr. Frankenstein pulled down to throw the juice to the monster, surging life through his body. As a kid who had to work in the asparagus fields, I remember my old man bringing the crew of us school kids up from the dusty, hot fields to get that cold drink of water that poured out of that pipe. Damn! That water was so pure, cold and quenched your thirst like nothing else could! God! What I wouldn't give for just one swallow of it!

I think about the last time I was in the hospital with hepatitis. I was in my home town and my buddy, Rick, would scale the side of the building and bring me fried chicken. Man, if he wasn't so far away, I *know* he would be here for me.

….I'm lonely….The morphine is not letting me deny that….I'm crying….

It is day three. I am awakened with the feeling of a loving touch, one I have felt all of my life. Both of her small, soft hands are gently holding my bandaged hand between hers, and I see Mom's tears running down her face as she asks, "How are you son?" I tell her I'm OK, that I just hurt. I helplessly watch her cry, unable to hug her. I see my Aunt Ick in the room. "Aunty Ick!", I beckon. Aunt Ick moves toward my bed and strokes my forehead. She asks me if I'm OK and I tell her I am and ask her how Mom's doing. Aunt Ick says Mom is not doing too well, that she's worried. I say, "I'm OK Aunty Ick. I'll get better! Hell, I'm not dead dammit! Aunty Ick, get me some food, their food tastes like shit! I'm starving!" Good old Aunt Ick reaches in her purse and gives me some candy. I knew she would come through. Mom is now stroking my forehead. Not much is said, as I drift in and out of my morphine state.

....Mom....my mommy....thank God you and Aunty Ick are here....oh mom, I'm so sorry....all my life I've given you nothing but worry and misery.... don't cry mom....I don't wanna see you cry mom....I just keep making you so worried....

The nurse walks in and snaps me out of my thoughts. I am pissed! Time to go down to the debris tank – that means it's the afternoon. I wonder how much time just went by. Mom says, "I'm staying with Aunt Ick. I'll be back in the morning. I love you son." I feel bad for Mom. I tell her OK, and that I love her. I tell Aunty Ick goodbye and she smiles and says, "Bye Rock." I feel a tingle of hope as Aunty Ick gets to the door, looks back at me and gives me a big wink. I will get out of this place – I will!

The preparation for Lucifer's "burn victim treatment" begins, but now I feel stronger. I can handle this better; I will see my mom again soon. I feel better now with the comfort Mom brought me. I feel stronger knowing she and Aunty Ick are nearby.

I must be getting better because I am getting bitchy! I can't take a crap because I can't wipe my own ass. I hate this damn hospital food. They keep trying to make me drink milk and I swore off that since I was a little kid. My cousin Kent squirted it in my mouth straight from the cow's udder! Blech!! All I want is something decent to eat, and to drink a Coke – or a *beer!* I can only use my phone when the nurse holds it to my good ear. I couldn't see visitors, but now that they're allowed to come, it won't stop! The frigging news media is constantly on my ass! I have learned to embrace the words "No comment". Hell, only a *fool* would make a statement while flowing with morphine thoughts, later to be printed for all to read. I would never do that – or did I? Shit! Tell them to *leave*! Just once I would like to use my phone without having to wipe my blood off of it. God! I can't even talk to my friends! My right ear has the top burned off. I'm using my left one, the better of the two – a little crispy, but still intact. Crap! Who was I just talking to? I open my eyes and the bloody phone is on the bed..... another "morphine moment".

The routine continues....morphine injection prior to the debris tank ordeal. I am a pin cushion between the morphine pokes and the blood-drawing vampires! I think they are using that blood for donations. There can't be any other explanation for taking all of my frigging blood! Blood suckers! If that isn't enough, I always get that one idiot nurse who just can't seem to find my vein! "OUCH! Give me the goddamn needle! I can hit a vein better than you!" Great! Now I've made her nervous and she misses again.

My mind goes back to the balloon and I can still see those poor bastards looking over the edge. I wonder how badly they were fried – were their eyeballs boiled out of their sockets in their skulls, with nothing but charred skeleton faces and remnants of dripping melted skin? I shake my head to get the gruesome thoughts out of it, but I know they will come back again.

After some time I notice my fingernails are turning black and falling off. Funny how I begin to use my body changes as a way to discern the amount of time I am here. Speaking of body changes, here comes that pretty nurse, the one who bathes me in the mornings. She is so nice, gentle and caring as she softly bathes my wounds. When she moves the sponge to the sore on my upper thigh, I find myself getting an erection. I am embarrassed because I cannot hide it. I tell her and she laughs. I think she likes it too. Hell! I can't even masturbate!

Jimmy and I are becoming pretty tight. The nurses tend to us at alternate times. I hear the poor kid's teeth grinding when his bandages are being removed. The sound is loud when it's the only sound in the room. We have this one nurse, a Jamaican woman, who comes in the afternoon to remove our bandages. This nurse does not use the spray bottle to soften the scabs and alleviate the bandage removal process, no, this bitch rips them off dry. I swear she enjoys seeing our pain as we wince, grimace and grind our teeth with the tearing of our skin. It's been several weeks of this afternoon "Jamaican torture", and I have had it! I decide to take matters into my own hands and let this woman know that I will no longer tolerate her abuse. I *had* to do this – more so for my young friend than for myself. After our morning treatment, I tell Jimmy, "Hey Jimmy! Watch what's gonna happen when that bitch tears my bandages off this afternoon." Jimmy asks me what I'm going to do. "You'll see" I answer.

Lunch is good for once! No milk, *two* juices, grilled cheese sandwich and tomato soup! Damn! A real meal! After lunch I drift into a deep sleep. It's been a long time since I've had a good sleep. I am awakened after some time by a nurse with the morphine shot. She asks me which side of my buttocks I want it in and I tell her it doesn't matter, that they both hurt. She sticks it in and I feel the liquid burn as she empties the syringe. "You're all set Rocky". I feel it coming on like it always does – like a train rolling down the tracks. My eyes are starting to droop, my saliva's drooling out of the corners of my mouth. I find myself looking forward to this damn drug .. I'm drifting into that dreamy mental state.

I hear Jimmy say, "Here she comes!" "Right on time", 'I'm thinking. She always goes to Jimmy first. She begins her usual routine, and I can almost *hear* the scabs being ripped off his wounds, but not as loud as the grinding sound of poor Jimmy's clenched teeth.

.....that fucking bitch....

I'm starting to come out of my morphine buzz – I'm feeling Jimmy's pain as she continues ripping off the puss-dried bandages. My little buddy is starting to cry and I can see that bitch's face. She appears to be enjoying herself! I hear her thick Jamaican accent – "Lay still boy – lay still!" I see the fresh blood on the once white gauze as she discards it.

....now it's my turn....c'mon you she-devil.... bring it on....ol' Rocco's ready for you bitch....

I'm looking at Jimmy's eyes, intently staring at me through his stocking holes. She pushes the stainless steel tray to the side of my bed. I spot that damn spray bottle, full of water, not a drop used on poor Jimmy. I am convinced that this bitch has no mercy. She lifts my left arm and I'm glad she does, because my right hand is not in a soft cast like my left hand, and I'm gonna need it. She cuts the end of the bandage and begins to unwind it, leaning closer as she moves up my arm.

….god that hurts....damn you....this is gonna stop!...

I pull my arm away and tell her to soak the damn bandages with water. She grabs my arm back, tells me to stay still, and resumes her Jamaican torture. I jerk my arm back again and tell her, "Look lady! Soak the bandages!" She says, "I know my job, don't tell me."

….ok lady, go ahead, do it again....

She grabs it again, I jerk my arm back and "Fuck you" flies out of my mouth. Then she said it – in her smart-ass tone of voice – "You Americans have life too good". For the <u>last</u> time she grabs my arm – my right hand bolts up and around her throat! I squeeze her throat tightly and pull her face close to mine. Her eyes are so huge they're bulging out of her head. It's *our* turn! I tell her through my gritted teeth, "Don't you **ever, ever** touch me or that boy again you bitch!" My hand releases her throat at the same time my arm pushes her away. She falls backward and lands on the floor, screaming at the top of her lungs like she just saw a ghost. Five or six nurses come running into the room, pick her up off the floor and rush her away. One upset nurse approaches me and asks me what just happened. I tell her nothing happened. She looks to Jimmy and asks him. Jimmy says he didn't see a thing.

Jimmy and I are alone now. In that silence, I look over at my hooded buddy and I see a smile through that mouth hole for the first time. I'm smiling myself, and as we share this victory, I assure him that she won't touch us again. He sounds relieved as he thanks me. I reply, "That's ok Jimmy, it was time. Thanks for not telling on me." He responded with a smile.

….good job Rocco….

Next morning a new doctor comes in. He's asking in this soft voice how things are going and how I'm feeling. I ask him who he is and he tells me he's a doctor. I say, "Oh yeah? What's your specialty?" He gives me some fancy-ass name for his profession, but I know what the hell he is – he fits the shoes perfectly – he's a damn shrink! Finally he asks me about yesterday's nurse incident. Aha! How quickly he reveals the sole purpose of his phony concern for me. I tell him, "She treated Jimmy and me like shit!" He asks me what I mean by that and I explain the Jamaican torture to him. He has the audacity to tell me that's no reason to do what I did. I respond, "Look doc, you're not in this bed like we are! Have you ever been burned?" He looks at me and bluntly responds, "Sure". I say, "What? With a little match or something? I'm talking *really* burned. Why don't you let me burn you time and time again in the same spot on your body and let's see how you do?! I'm sure you'll pull back! I'm sure you'll finally try to make me stop giving you pain. It frigging hurts! You see that boy? Well, you lie in this room day after day and listen to him cry and grind his teeth in agony while that bitch tears off his bandages without soaking the crusty scabs first. Oh yeah! And while you're here, doc, why don't you stick around and watch our pleasant saunas!"

So this brainiac tells me 'he's wondering why I'm not grieving the death of my friend'. I say, "What do you mean?" Then he responds, saying that he heard I'm telling everyone that when I get out of here I'm gonna skydive again. I say, "Yeah, why not?" He asks me if I have a death wish. I'm looking at this idiot wondering how much he's gonna stick it to me for this joke of a session. I decide to respond and try to enlighten the fool. "Look doc, I'm here because I'm a skydiver with good training and skills that instinctively enabled me to get out of that basket and fall 100 feet and not break a bone in my body. A *death wish* – where does that come into the picture?" He replies, "Why, skydiving is very dangerous!" I am getting defensive now, defensive and pissed at this know-it-all prick! "You don't have a clue what you're talking about! You have no education of my sport – no knowledge of the equipment, the training, the airplane – nothing – not one damn thing! Hell! You don't even know the fatality statistics that come into play when you rate this sport as dangerous. You come in here, ignorant to everything we just talked about. Why don't you do me a favor and do your frigging homework before you come back in here and try to 'figure me out'! I know you're a shrink – aren't you?!"

He answers that he is and that he was sent because I choked a nurse. I retort, "Yeah! Well, pal, I can't be that crazy because that boy and I don't have to suffer at the evil hands of her anymore. Besides, she told me she hated Americans and I'm <u>proud</u> to be an American! I competed in two World Championships and carried gold medals home to my country. My father fought for this country, for our freedom to make choices – choices like the one I made yesterday. Let me tell you, my friend, it was the *only* choice I had for me and Jimmy. So, why don't you run along now and kick our conversation around and then write your little report. You're the one who needs help – you're so shallow!" The poor sap turns around and walks away. I laugh to myself.

….what an idiot ….sad ….so sad….they make way too much money….he's probably from 1st ward….

The day finally came when they took out my tubes, and it felt great to be unplugged and free to move around. I could take care of my bathroom needs and get around ok. Mom and Aunty Ick were visiting me regularly and I was enjoying the hamburgers and cokes that Aunty Ick managed to smuggle in for me. Mom was feeling better because she could see that I was getting better. The doc told me that I would never have full mobility of my hands. Don't ever tell me never! I now have full mobility, thanks to self-rehabilitation and my stubborn determination. I had been in there a good month, and one day after examining me the doc said I could probably be out the next week or so. I told him it would be good to get out and have a cold beer. He said, "Why wait? You can have one now if you want." I was shocked! Doc told me that beer is high in protein and ok for me to have. Go figure! Well, Jimmy's dad overheard the conversation and showed up the very next night with a 12-pack of

Bud. I spent the next few nights drinking my cold beer and looking forward to my release.
 ….life ain't so bad after all God….

About the Author

Rocky Evans, born March 22, 1952, experienced his first parachute jump in May of 1970, and excelled to the level of achieving World Championship Skydiving awards three times. The author was an integral part of the team that pioneered the Accelerated Free Fall Skydiving training technique. This AFF training technique has been implemented all over the world, and included students such as former President George Bush, Sr., Matthew Modine and Tom Cruise. In 1985 Rocky was recruited by the British Broadcasting Corporation to be part of a team on a documentary for NOVA entitled, "Skydive into the Rain Forest". Adding to his memorable experiences, Rocky skydived tandem with a 67-year old woman onto the North Pole in 1996. An experienced skydiver with 8,300 jumps to his credit, Rocky also maintains a commercial pilot's license with 3,300 hours of flying on his log, along with being a licensed FAA Senior Rigger and FAA Authorized Inspector. Seasoned in most aspects of the aviation industry, Rocky Evans has written the story, "TRUTH".